This book belongs to

....

....

GRAFFEG

The Versatile Reptile
Published by Graffeg Limited © 2023.

Text © 2023 Nicola Davies. Illustrations © 2023 Abbie Cameron. Designed and produced by Graffeg.

Graffeg Limited, 24 Stradey Park Business Centre, Mwrwg Road, Llangennech, Llanelli, Carmarthenshire, SA14 8YP, Wales, UK. Tel 01554 824000. www.graffeg.com.

Nicola Davies is hereby identified as the author of this work in accordance with section 77 of the Copyright, Designs and Patents Act 1988.

A CIP Catalogue record for this book is available from the British Library.

All rights reserved. No part of this publication may be reproduced, stored in a retrieval system or transmitted, in any form or by any means, electronic, mechanical, photocopying, recording or otherwise, without the prior permission of the publishers.

ISBN 9781912213689

Printed in China

1 2 3 4 5 6 7 8 9

THE VERSATILE REPTILE

Written by
Nicola Davies

Illustrated by
Abbie Cameron

Most people say reptiles are weird and should be universally feared...

They'll talk about a deadly bite,

Or massive coils to squeeze you tight.

But there's nothing
quite so versatile
As the creatures
that we call...

REPTILE!

Let's start with that coat of scales,

Tough as armour or chain mail.

Each scale can be a different hue,

So they stand out... or hide from view.

They can run

and climb

Some have taken to the sky,
Though what they do is glide, not fly.

No, there's nothing quite so versatile
As the creatures that we call...

Reptiles can live in every spot,
Especially ones that are quite hot.

They move about on scorching sand,
By swapping feet round when they stand.

Or live in jungles, high in trees,

Or roam around the wide blue seas.

Most eat beetles, bugs and ants.

But some eat fruit and munch on plants.

One dives down deep where seaweed grows,

From crocodiles

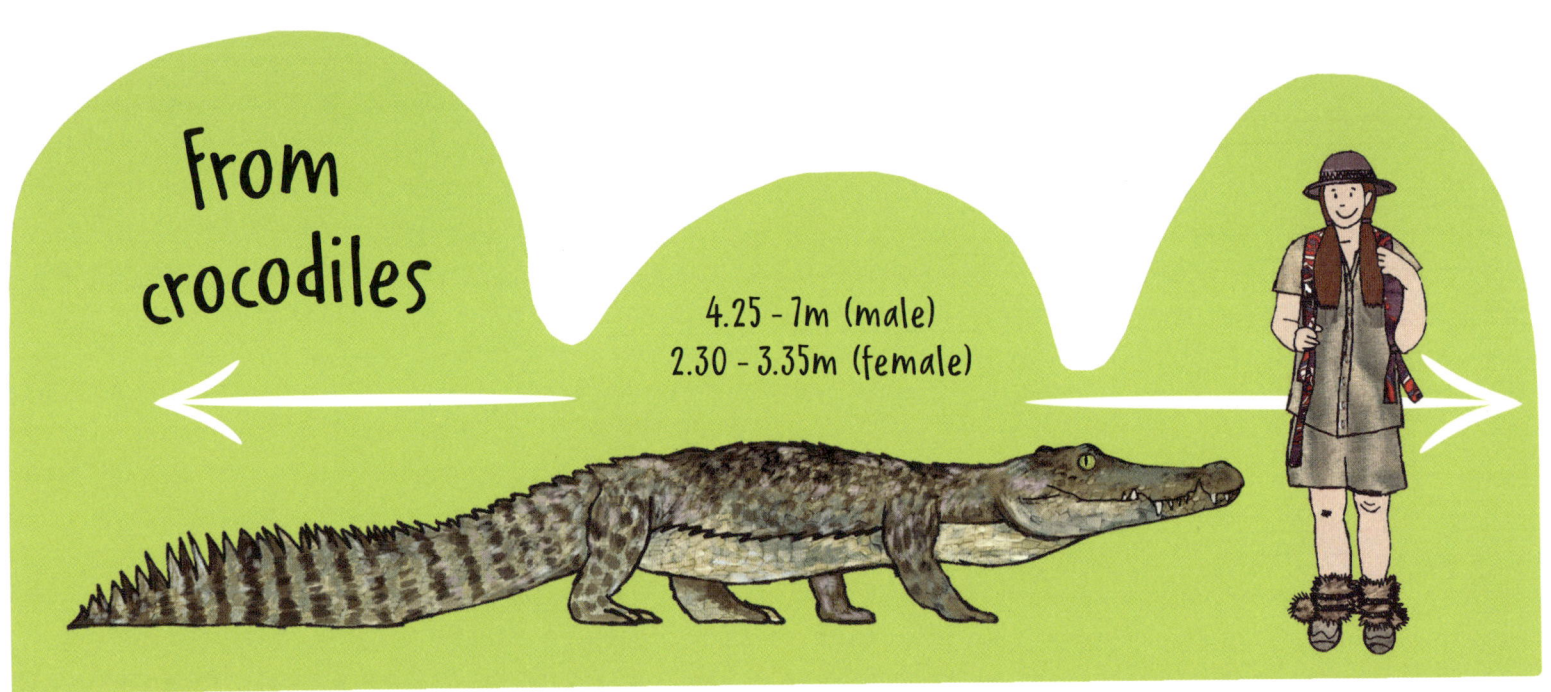

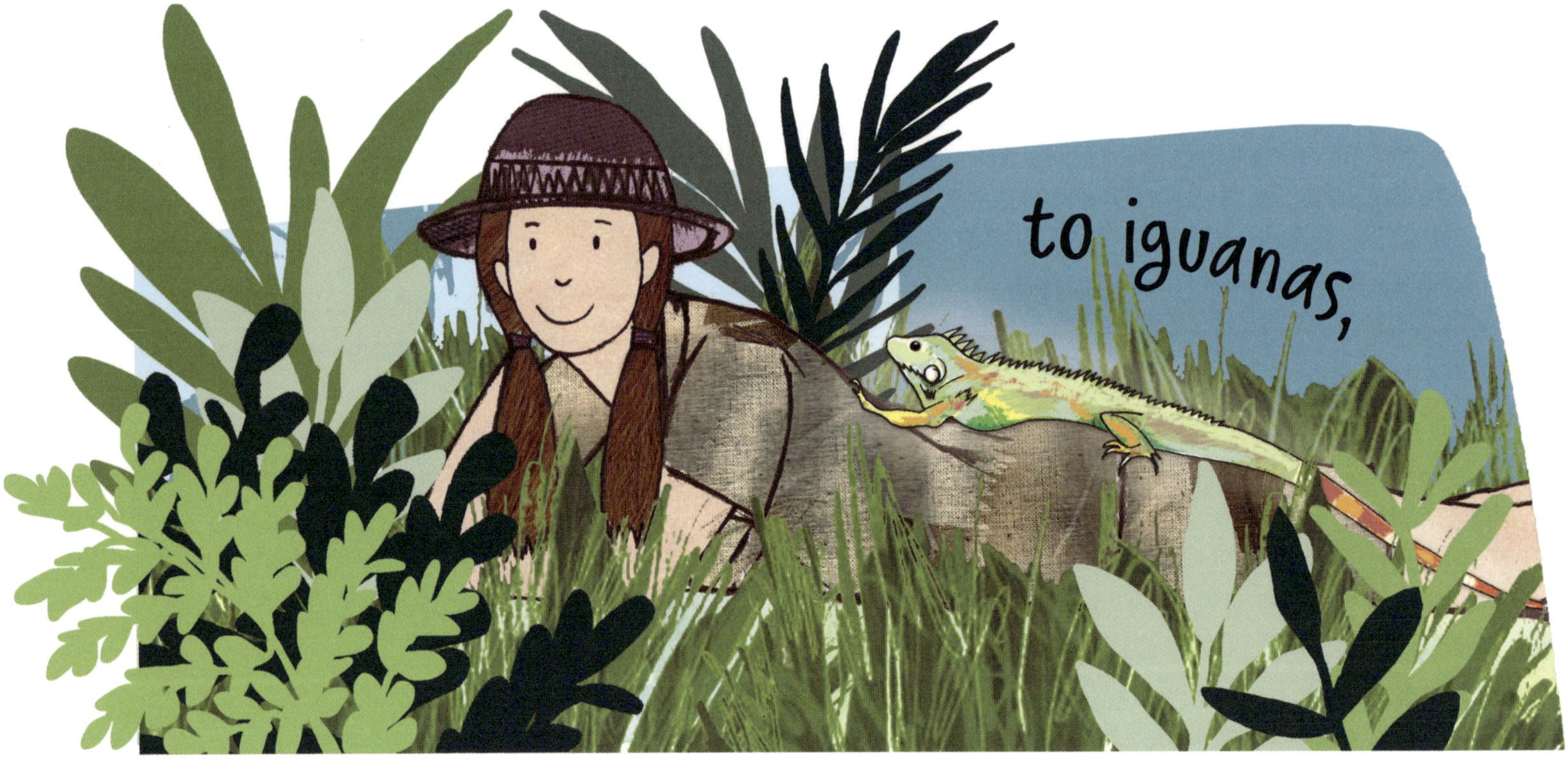

to iguanas,

From monster sized to quite minute,
From grim and gross to super cute.
There's nothing quite as versatile
as the creatures that we call...

PUZZLE TO FINISH

Solutions: 1E, 2B, 3A, 4C, 5D

Nicola Davies

Nicola is an award-winning author, whose many books for children include *The Promise* (Green Earth Book Award 2015, CILIP Kate Greenaway Shortlist 2015), *Tiny* (AAAS Subaru Prize 2015), *A First Book of Nature*, *Whale Boy* (Blue Peter Award Shortlist 2014), and the *Heroes of the Wild* series (Portsmouth Book Prize 2014). She graduated in Zoology, studied whales and bats and then worked for the BBC Natural History Unit. Underlying all Nicola's writing is the belief that a relationship with nature is essential to every human being, and that now, more than ever, we need to renew that relationship. Nicola's children's books from Graffeg include *Perfect* (CILIP Kate Greenaway Longlist 2017), *The Pond* (CILIP Kate Greenaway Longlist 2018), the Shadows and Light series and the Animal Surprises series.

Abbie Cameron

Abbie Cameron was raised on the farmlands of the West Country. Surrounded by nature, she developed a love and appreciation for all creatures great and small.
Abbie studied Illustration at University of Wales Trinity Saint David, where she first met Nicola Davies. Her style is playful and inventive, sharing some of the tongue-in-cheek attitude and doodle-like style of other contemporary British illustrators. She employs the use of bright colours and texture whilst playing with scale, composition and open space.
Abbie's other books include *Animal Surprises* (The Klaus Flugge Prize for the Most Exciting Newcomer to Picture Book Illustration Longlist 2017), *The Word Bird* and *Into the Blue*, as well as their companion series of How to Draw books. Abbie was also highly commended in the Penguin Random House Design Awards 2014.

Rhyming Book Series

Discover the delights of nature with zoologist and top children's author Nicola Davies. Follow the young adventurer as she treks through the jungle in *Animal Surprises*, dives deep down into the sea in *Into the Blue*, climbs up high into the trees in *The Word Bird*, discovers the wonders hidden inside eggs of all shapes and sizes in *The Secret of the Egg* and journeys around the world to uncover the world of spiders, mini-beasts and more in *Invertebrates are Cool!*. Each rhyming book is fully illustrated in colour by Abbie Cameron.

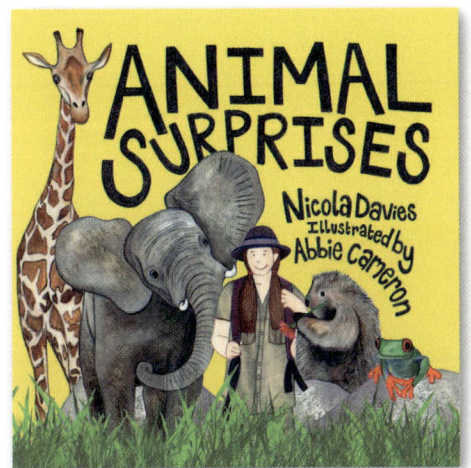

Animal Surprises
ISBN 9781910862445

The Word Bird
ISBN 9781910862438

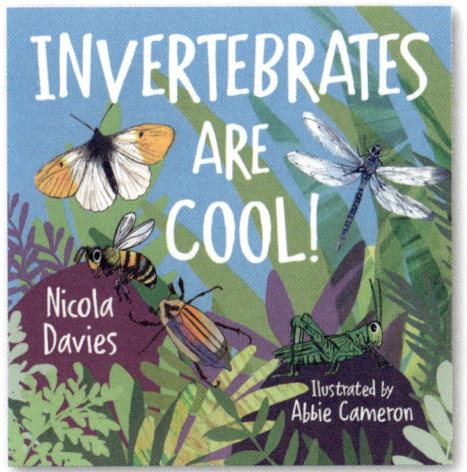

Invertebrates are Cool!
ISBN 9781912213696

Into the Blue
ISBN 9781910862452

The Secret of the Egg
ISBN 9781912213672

www.graffeg.com

How to Draw Series

In this companion series, Abbie Cameron teaches children how to draw their favourite animals from the rhyming books step-by-step, alongside informative text about each species from Nicola Davies.

Titles in the series:
- Animal Surprises: How to Draw
- The Word Bird: How to Draw
- Into the Blue: How to Draw

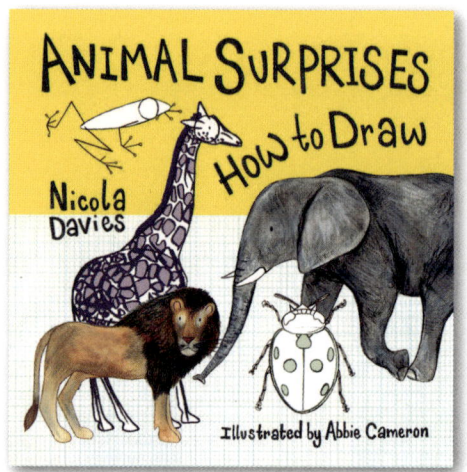

Animal Surprises: How to Draw
ISBN 9781912050567

The Word Bird: How to Draw
ISBN 9781912050574

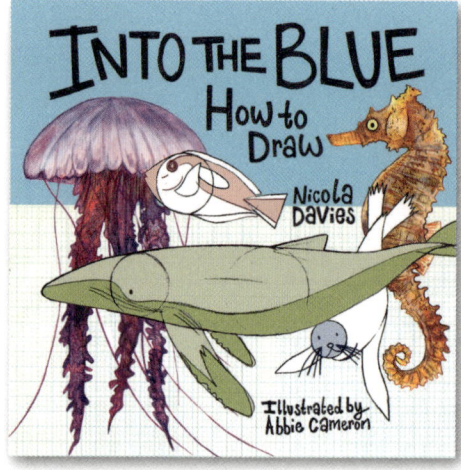

Into the Blue: How to Draw
ISBN 9781912050550

Visit **graffeg.com/pages/how-to-draw** to watch Abbie drawing some of the animals from the series with step-by-step instructions.

www.graffeg.com